ALL AROUND THE WORLD
HUNGARY

by Kristine Spanier, MLIS

Ideas for Parents and Teachers

Pogo Books let children practice reading informational text while introducing them to nonfiction features such as headings, labels, sidebars, maps, and diagrams, as well as a table of contents, glossary, and index.

Carefully leveled text with a strong photo match offers early fluent readers the support they need to succeed.

Before Reading

- "Walk" through the book and point out the various nonfiction features. Ask the student what purpose each feature serves.
- Look at the glossary together. Read and discuss the words.

Read the Book

- Have the child read the book independently.
- Invite him or her to list questions that arise from reading.

After Reading

- Discuss the child's questions. Talk about how he or she might find answers to those questions.
- Prompt the child to think more. Ask: Hungary has many thermal lakes. What landforms are where you live?

Pogo Books are published by Jump!
5357 Penn Avenue South
Minneapolis, MN 55419
www.jumplibrary.com

Library of Congress Cataloging-in-Publication Data

Names: Spanier, Kristine, author.
Title: Hungary / by Kristine Spanier, MLIS.
Description: Minneapolis, MN: Jump!, Inc., [2022]
Series: All around the world
Includes index. | Audience: Ages 7-10
Identifiers: LCCN 2020051614 (print)
LCCN 2020051615 (ebook)
ISBN 9781636900025 (hardcover)
ISBN 9781636900032 (paperback)
ISBN 9781636900049 (ebook)
Subjects: LCSH: Hungary—Juvenile literature.
Classification: LCC DB906 .S63 2022 (print)
LCC DB906 (ebook) | DDC 943.9—dc23
LC record available at https://lccn.loc.gov/2020051614
LC ebook record available at https://lccn.loc.gov/2020051615

Editor: Jenna Gleisner
Designer: Molly Ballanger

Photo Credits: V_E/Shutterstock, cover; Frog Dares/Shutterstock, 1; Pixfiction/Shutterstock, 3; Ikonya/iStock, 4; Skovalsky/Dreamstime, 5; Gudella/iStock, 6-7; David Havel/Shutterstock, 8; Tom Kolossa/Shutterstock, 8-9; Richard Semik/Shutterstock, 10; Csaba Der/Dreamstime, 11; Nikolay Antonov/Shutterstock, 12-13; Gabor Tokodi/Shutterstock, 14-15; GSDesign/Shutterstock, 16 (top); Alexander Mychko/Dreamstime, 16 (bottom); Fanniframboise/Dreamstime, 17; AP Images, 18-19; Nano Calvo/age fotostock/SuperStock, 20-21; offstocker/Shutterstock, 23.

Printed in the United States of America at Corporate Graphics in North Mankato, Minnesota.

TABLE OF CONTENTS

CHAPTER 1

LAND OF WONDERS

Would you like to swim in a **thermal** lake? Hungary has more than 1,300 thermal **springs**. People soak and swim in them!

Hungary is in Central Europe. The Mátra Mountains are in the north. Mount Kékes is the highest point. It is 3,327 feet (1,014 meters) high.

stalagmite $\cdots\cdots\blacktriangleright$

The Aggtelek Caves are near the border of Slovakia. They make up the largest **stalactite** cave system in Europe. **Stalagmites** form in the caves, too.

DID YOU KNOW?

The Aggtelek Caves consist of hundreds of caves! You can visit them.

A **national park** is in the Hortobágy region. This is in the east. It is the largest natural grassland in Central Europe. Wild horses roam. Birds **migrate** here. They feed and rest.

cranes

grassland

CHAPTER 2

VILLAGES AND CITIES

Hollókő Castle

Hollókő is an old village in the north. Visitors can see what homes and buildings looked like in the 1600s. You can also see a castle that has been around since at least 1310!

apricot

Kecskemét is called the **orchard** of Hungary. Much of the country's fruit is grown here. Apricots are made into jellies and syrups. Some say these are the best apricots in Europe! Hírös Hét is a **festival**. It celebrates the **harvest**.

The **capital** is Budapest. A prime minister leads the government. Lawmakers meet in the parliament building.

The Danube River flows through Budapest. This is the second longest river in Europe. It is 1,777 miles (2,860 kilometers) long.

Hungarian Parliament Building

TAKE A LOOK!

Hungary has a **coat of arms**. What do its parts stand for? Take a look!

CROWN:
Holy Crown of King Stephen I, Hungary's first king

FOUR WHITE STRIPES:
the Danube, Tisza, Drava, and Sava Rivers

GREEN HILLS:
mountains

Danube River

Esztergom was the birthplace of King Stephen I in the late 900s. Many kings made this city their home until the 1200s.

The Basilica of Esztergom is the largest church in Hungary. It took 47 years to build. From the top, you can see Slovakia!

WHAT DO YOU THINK?

Slovakia borders Hungary. What country is closest to yours? Can you see it from your town or city?

Basilica of Esztergom

CHAPTER 3

LIFE IN HUNGARY

Try goulash! This is a beef stew. Chicken paprikash is chicken in a paprika sauce. Many meals are served with noodles.

goulash

chicken paprikash

Winters here are cool. But summers are warm enough for swimming! Lake Balaton is the largest lake in Central Europe. People kayak, sail, and windsurf on this lake.

Many children here go to preschool. Everyone must go to school by age six. They attend until they are 16 years old. Some students move on to high school. This prepares them for college. Others attend **trade school**. Almost everyone learns a second language.

St. Stephen's Day is August 20. It celebrates King Stephen I. Easter is another popular holiday. People come together in their villages. They dance, sing, and eat.

There is so much to see in Hungary. Would you like to visit?

WHAT DO YOU THINK?

What holidays do you celebrate? Who do you celebrate them with?

QUICK FACTS & TOOLS

HUNGARY

Location: Central Europe

Size: 35,919 square miles (93,030 square kilometers)

Population: 9,771,827 (July 2020 estimate)

Capital: Budapest

Type of Government: parliamentary republic

Languages: Hungarian, English, German

Exports: machinery and equipment, food products

Currency: Hungarian forint

capital: A city where government leaders meet.

coat of arms: A design on a shield that identifies a noble family or person, a city, or an organization.

festival: A celebration or holiday.

harvest: The gathering of crops that are ready to eat.

migrate: To move from one region or habitat to another.

national park: A large section of land that is protected by the government.

orchard: An area of land where fruit or nut trees are grown.

springs: Places where water rises to the surface from underground sources.

stalactite: An icicle-shaped mineral deposit that hangs from the roof of a cave.

stalagmites: Tapering columns that stick up from cave floors.

thermal: Of or having to do with heat.

trade school: A school where students learn a particular trade or craft, especially one that requires working with the hands or with machines.

Hungary's currency

INDEX

TO LEARN MORE

Finding more information is as easy as 1, 2, 3.

❶ Go to www.factsurfer.com

❷ Enter "Hungary" into the search box.

❸ Choose your book to see a list of websites.

FACT SURFER